ROYAL ROMANCE, Modern marriagE

 The Love Story of William & Kate

Mary Boone

TRIUMPH
BOOKS

Triumph Books and colophon are registered trademarks of Random House, Inc.

This book is available in quantity at special discounts for your group or organization. For further information, contact:
Triumph Books
542 South Dearborn Street
Suite 750
Chicago, Illinois 60605
(312) 939-3330
Fax (312) 663-3557
www.triumphbooks.com

Printed in U.S.A.
ISBN: 978-1-60078-605-1

Design and page production by Andrew Burwell
Project Management by Rockett Media

All photos courtesy Getty Images.

ROYAL ROMANCE, Modern marriagE

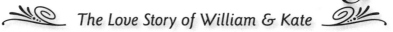

The Love Story of William & Kate

THE LOVE STORY OF WILLIAM AND KATE

The 2011 royal wedding of Prince William and Kate Middleton will be a state occasion filled with enormous pomp and ceremony. The fairytale-come-true is certain to attract global interest, with every detail of the courtship and engagement having been reported by the media for months. What does the dress look like? Who's on the guest list? What music will be played at the wedding?

Announcement of the royal engagement ended years of speculation about the couple's future. But this story actually began years ago, long before William's boarding school years or military service; before Kate modeled that now-famous sheer dress in a charity fashion show and yes, before the couple met at college.

Within these pages, you'll read the individual stories of William and Kate: their births, their family lives, their schooling. You'll discover what influenced their personalities and interests and, it will become clear, what brought these two very different souls together.

Theirs is an unlikely but authentic romance, worthy of celebration.

CHAPTER ONE:

A Prince is Born

CHAPTER ONE: A Prince is Born

At age 13, Prince William was attending Ludgrove, a boarding school in rural Berkshire, England, where he shared a room with four other boys. He was rugby and hockey team captain, played basketball and footie (that's soccer to you Americans), and represented the school at cross-country running.

He was like every other teenage boy. Except that he, someday, will be King.

William Arthur Philip Louis was born at 9:03 p.m. on June 21, 1982, to Charles, Prince of Wales, and Diana, Princess of Wales. The public was hungry for every detail of his life from the very beginning. The entrance to St. Mary's Hospital had been occupied by photographers and onlookers for days and newspapers around the world had been on "baby watch" for months.

"I believe that the whole of England lay with me during labor," Diana later told an interviewer.

William's birth capped a very difficult pregnancy and delivery. The Princess was exhausted but thrilled to be holding a sweet baby boy – an heir to throne – in her arms. Her hospital room filled with a sea of roses, she could hear supporters' cheers from outside: "Long live Diana!"

Princess Diana and her newborn son stayed in the hospital just one day before going home, where a nanny and infant nurse helped care for tiny William. Diana, Charles and Wills, as he became affectionately known, quickly grew into a loving family.

Shortly after his son was born, Charles wrote to a friend: "He really does look surprisingly appetizing and has sausage fingers just like mine."

When Wills was just 9 months old, his parents had to make an official state visit to Australia. The trip was to last six weeks – such a long time that Diana said she simply couldn't leave her baby behind. She insisted on taking William along and explained her position to the Queen who quickly refused

The Prince and Princess of Wales leave London's St. Mary's Hospital after the birth of their baby, Prince William.

Diana actively cared for her boys, relying as little as possible on nannies and nurses. Here, the young princes and their mother enjoy a sleigh ride during a 1994 ski holiday in Austria.

her request. Diana then threatened to stay home, in London, with her son. The Queen knew the Australian people would be hugely disappointed if Charles came without Diana so, after considerable thought, she allowed it.

The Australian trip was a success. The Prince and Princess toured every state in the continent, taking a break every three or four days to visit William who was staying at a sheep ranch with his nanny. The schedule was made more difficult because of the baby, but it also allowed for special family time.

"The great joy was that we were totally alone together," Charles wrote home in a letter to friends.

On September 15, 1984, England's Royal Family grew by one when Henry "Harry" Charles Albert David was born. Royal-watchers worried about how Prince William, then 2 years old, would react to his new baby brother. They got their answer when Charles brought the toddler to the hospital the morning after Harry was born. Diana heard William running down the hall and got out of bed to make introductions. William was allowed to touch his brother and hold his hand. William reportedly was gentle and immediately quite pleased with the baby.

"It will be lovely for William to have a companion and a playmate, and someone to fight with," Diana's father, Earl Spencer, told reporters at the time. "I'm sure Harry will be a very good chap."

Charles and Diana worked tirelessly to ensure their boys' childhoods were as normal as possible – considering their blood-

CROWN JEWELS

When William does become King, he will rule over Great Britain – and so much more.

Currently, Elizabeth II is Queen of the United Kingdom (Great Britain and Northern Ireland), Canada, Australia, New Zealand, Jamaica, Barbados, the Bahamas, Grenada, Papua New Guinea, the Solomon Islands, Tuvalu, Saint Lucia, Saint Vincent and the Grenadines, Antigua and Barbuda, Belize, and Saint Kitts and Nevis, where she is represented by Governors-General. The sixteen countries over which she reigns are known as Commonwealth Realms.

The British monarchy is known as a constitutional monarchy which means that, while the King or Queen is the head of State, the ability to make and pass legislation belongs to an elected Parliament.

So, while the Queen – and someday, William as the King – has no political role, the Sovereign acts as a focus for national identity, unity and pride; gives a sense of stability and continuity; officially recognizes success and excellence; and supports the ideal of voluntary service.

lines and the fact that they had bodyguards and photographers following them almost everywhere they went.

When he was 7, William told his mother he wanted to be a police offer when he

CHAPTER ONE: A Prince is Born

Dramatically different parenting styles created friction between Charles and Diana.

grew up so he could protect her. Before Diana could even respond, his brother is reported to have said: "No, you can't. You've got to be King."

Diana was both a devoted mother and active playmate for her boys, roller skating with them down the long hallways in Kensington Palace and using bed sheets to dress up like ghosts. Prince Charles thought that, instead of playing childish games, the boys should become comfortable with their future royal duties as soon as possible; he insisted on strict discipline and proper manners. This clash in parenting styles created friction between Charles and Diana.

William attended Mrs. Mynors School as a pre-schooler and then Wetherby School, a public school in London, from 1987 to 1990. He was the first royal prince to attend an ordinary primary school, rather than being educated at home.

While boarding schools are commonplace for the children of dignitaries and high society, Princess Diana was saddened by the notion of having her eldest child move away from home. She loved her son and knew she would miss having him around Kensington Palace. Still, William enrolled at Ludgrove School in 1990, staying there until July 1995.

Always one for a game of soccer or basketball, it should be no surprise that William suffered a sports injury while at Ludgrove. In 1991, he got clocked in the head with a seven iron. The golf club injury required stitches and left the prince with what he refers to as his "Harry Potter scar."

"I call it that because it glows sometimes and some people notice it, and some people don't notice it at all," he said in an ABC News interview.

It was also while he was at Ludgrove that Charles and Diana separated, forcing William and Harry to divide their time between their parents' homes when they were not in school. Charles often spent his time with the boys outdoors, hunting or hiking. Diana preferred to travel with her sons, often heading to Switzerland to ski or to a secluded beach in the Caribbean for swimming and sunbathing.

William enrolled at the prestigious Eton College in July 1995, studying geography, biology and art history.

He was 15-years-old when his world was turned upside down. His beloved mother was killed in a car crash in Paris on August 31, 1997. Despite enormous grief, William helped make arrangements for his mother's funeral; it reportedly was his idea to ask Elton John to sing "Candle in the Wind" at the service. Both William and Harry walked in the funeral processional, following the carriage carrying Diana's coffin. It's a period of his life that he still prefers not to discuss.

After completing his studies at Eton, the Prince took a gap year (a common name for a break in schooling), during which he took

SUCCESSION TO THE THRONE

Queen Elizabeth II became Queen of the United Kingdom on February 6, 1952. She has reigned for more than 59 years.

Who will replace the Queen when she steps down? That's a matter of some speculation but there are many regulations in place that help decide who will succeed her. The law, for example, states that only Protestant heirs of Princess Sophia, may succeed to the throne. Catholics, those who marry Catholics, and those born to unmarried parents are specifically disallowed from becoming king or queen.

Two recent polls in Britain reveal that the British public would prefer Prince William become the country's next king – not his father, Prince Charles, who is next in line to the throne. Prince William, however, says he has no interest in cheating his father of a chance to be king. William, in fact, has decided to remain in active military duty for now.

THE LINE OF SUCCESSION
1. Prince Charles of Wales, born 1948
2. Prince William of Wales, born 1982
3. Prince Henry of Wales, born 1984
4. Prince Andrew, the Duke of York, born 1960
5. Princess Beatrice of York, born 1988
6. Princess Eugenie of York, born 1990
7. Prince Edward, the Earl of Wessex, born 1964
8. James Alexander Philip Theo, Viscount Severn, born 2007
9. The Lady Louise Mountbatten-Windsor, born 2003
10. Anne, the Princess Royal, born 1950
11. Mr. Peter Phillips, born 1977
12. Miss Savannah Phillips, born 2010
13. Miss Zara Phillips, born 1981
14. David Albert Charles Armstrong-Jones, Viscount Linley, born 1961
15. The Honorable Charles Armstrong-Jones, born 1999
16. The Honorable Margarita Armstrong-Jones, born 2002
17. The Lady Sarah Chatto, born 1964
18. Master Samuel Chatto, born 1996
19. Master Arthur Chatto, born 1964
20. Prince Richard, the 2nd Duke of Gloucester, born 1944

CHAPTER ONE: A Prince is Born

liam joined the Royal Military Academy Sandhurst as an Officer Cadet. He was commissioned as an army officer in front of his grandmother, the Queen, in December 2006 and joined the Household Cavalry (Blues and Royals) as a Second Lieutenant.

In April 2008, the Queen appointed William to be a Royal Knight Companion of the Most Noble Order of the Garter; his installation ceremony was held at Windsor Castle.

part in military training exercises in Belize and taught children in Chile.

Upon returning to the United Kingdom and building on his already impressive education, Prince William chose to study at St. Andrews University in Fife, Scotland. It was while he was a St. Andrews that he first met the lovely Kate Middleton.

William initially intended to study art history while at St. Andrews but later changed his major. In 2005, he earned his Scottish Master of Arts degree with honors in geography.

After a period of work experience, Wil-

In 2009, William transferred to the Royal Air Force, was promoted to flight lieutenant and underwent helicopter flying training with the aim of becoming a full time pilot with the Search and Rescue Force. With his helicopter training completed, he is now at Royal Air Force (RAF) Valley, performing co-pilot duties on the Sea King search and rescue helicopter.

Now, this officer, gentleman, and future king has found the love of his life in Catherine Elizabeth Middleton.

ROYAL BROTHER, PRINCE HARRY

Prince Henry Charles Albert David – affectionately known as Prince Harry – was born September 15, 1984, at St. Mary's Hospital in central London. Known as the "Happy Prince" because of his propensity for smiling, he is third in the line of succession to the throne.

Prince Harry is and always has been

close to his older brother; the two have the shared experience of living life in the public eye.

Harry's education and upbringing were similar to William's. Harry attended Mrs. Mynors School, then Wetherby School in London. In September 1992, he joined his older brother at Ludgrove School in Berkshire; in 1998 he enrolled at Eton College.

During his gap year, Harry visited Australia, Argentina and Africa, where he made a documentary film about the plight of orphans in Lesotho.

In May 2005, Harry entered the Royal Military Academy. He successfully completed his training as an Officer Cadet and was commissioned in April 2006 as a Second Lieutenant in the Household Cavalry (Blues and Royals). In 2008, he served two months in Afghanistan with the British Army. In April 2008, he was promoted from Second Lieutenant to Lieutenant.

In January 2009, he began his training to become a fully operational, full-time Army Air Corps helicopter pilot. He remains an officer in the Household Cavalry during the training.

Beginning in his late teens, Prince Harry's sometimes unprincely behavior has made him the focus of countless tabloid reports.

He quickly earned a reputation as a playboy and was often photographed kissing girls he'd just met in bars. In 2002, at age 17, Clarence House admitted Harry had been caught drinking while under age and that he'd also smoked marijuana. In 2005, he was photographed wearing a home-made Swastika on his arm while at a friend's costume party. He's been in public scuffles with paparazzi, been accused of cheating on college coursework, and issued apologies for racist comments he's made.

Troubles aside, Prince William praised his brother in a 2010 interview with the (London) *Daily Mail*: "I think Harry's got a very free spirit and a very intuitive way of dealing with things, looking at problems … He's got a big heart and he wants to make a difference."

CHAPTER TWO:

Kate the Commoner

CHAPTER TWO: Kate the Commoner

Kate Middleton is not a member of nobility or aristocracy, which makes her a most unusual bride for the man who will likely be King.

Prince William's mother, Prince Diana, was the daughter of an Earl. Prince Andrew's ex-wife, Sarah Ferguson, had a great-grandfather who was a Duke.

Kate's parents run a mail-order company, making her the first commoner in line to become queen since Anne Hyde wed the Duke of York, later James II, in 1660.

Yes, Kate Middleton is a commoner who suddenly finds herself in a very uncommon position: She is marrying Prince William, heir to the British throne.

Catherine "Kate" Elizabeth Middleton was born January 9,

1982, at Royal Berkshire Hospital in Reading, Berkshire, England, to parents Carol and Michael Middleton. Carole Goldsmith Middleton is a builder's daughter from Southall, Middlesex. Michael Middleton, son of an airplane pilot, was born in Leeds. The two met in the mid-1970s while working as flight attendants for British Airlines.

CHAPTER TWO: Kate the Commoner

"Kate is an absolutely phenomenal girl – really popular, talent, creative and sporty." – **Former classmate Charlie Leslie**

Several years later, Michael was promoted to the role of flight dispatcher for British Airlines at Heathrow Airport, where he monitored the airline's fleet on the ground.

In 1979, the couple bought a modest home in Bradfield Southend, a village near Reading. They married in 1980 and their first child, Kate, was born two years later. Soon, the Middleton family grew to include another daughter, Philippa "Pippa," born in 1983, and a son, James, born in 1987. Kate's childhood was typical of others of the era. She loved to dance, play "musical statues" with her siblings, and dress up like a clown. Her favorite childhood birthday memory, she revealed recently, was "the amazing white rabbit marshmallow cake Mummy made when I was seven."

Anxious to spend more time with their children, Michael and Carole Middleton decided to start their own business, something that would allow them to work from home. In 1987, they founded Party Pieces, selling toys and games from a converted barn near their home.

Yvonne Cowdrey, the family's housekeeper at the time, told *The (London) Mail*:

"Carole was fed-up making up bags full of little gifts for the kids to take away from parties, and she realized other mums must feel the same. So, she thought it would be a good idea to start a business that sold ready-made party bags."

Both Michael and Carole worked long hours to get the business off the ground while their children studied at St. Andrew's School, Pangbourne, a nearby prep school. Kate attended classes there until she was 13

The Middletons' home business grew steadily, relying at first on in-person and catalog orders (Kate and Pippa often modeled merchandise in the catalogues). Soon, Party Pieces had an online presence, allowing it to sell goods to a larger audience. The family's thriving business meant they could, in 1995, buy a larger, more modern house in the neighboring village of Bucklebury. It also meant their children could attend Marlborough College, an expensive and exclusive school in Wiltshire.

Kate was a bright student, whose athleticism helped her shine in swimming, hockey, tennis, basketball and badminton. She earned the school record in her age group for the high jump. Said one school friend: "There was hardly a sport she didn't play."

Another former classmate, Charlie Leslie, told the British Broadcasting Corp. (BBC): "Kate is an absolutely phenomenal girl – really popular, talented, creative and sporty. She was captain of the school hockey team and played in the first pair at tennis."

A college master said: "I don't think you'd find anyone in Marlborough with a bad word to say about her. She excelled in all her subjects and was an A-grade pupil

WILLIAM'S PAST LOVES

The handsome, athletic and very princely William never had much of a problem finding girls to date. A few of the more notable beauties who've caught the Prince's eye include:

Isabella Anstruther-Gough-Calthorpe: This Society girl was allegedly seen in deep conversation with Wills at a 2005 charity ball, while Kate sat at a different table. The prince allegedly ignored Kate in favor of spending the evening with Isabella. On another occasion, William was reportedly seen kissing Isabella at a nightclub.

Elouise Blair: This Australian model was seen kissing William after meeting him at a party for Prince Harry. Any relationship was short lived.

Jecca (Jessica) Craig: This party events manager is said to have had a "pretend engagement" with William during his gap year travels. Her family owns a 55,000-acre game reserve in Kenya.

Davina Duckworth Chad: The media reports that William left Kate behind in Scotland to rendezvous with this older woman, actually a distant cousin, in London.

Rose Ferquhar: This aspiring actress has known William since they were children. The daughter of Captain Ian Farquhar, master of the Beaufort Hunt, reportedly stole William's heart after he left Eton College in 2000.

Olivia Hunt: She dated William at St. Andrews – and knew Kate as a fellow student. The three have apparently remained friends. Olivia went on to date William van Cutsem, son of Prince Charles' friend High van Cutsem; the two have since parted ways.

William's former girlfriend, Arabella Musgrave, arrives at a party in 2003.

Arabella Musgrave: The only girlfriend prior to Kate to actually be acknowledged by the Royal Family, Arabella allegedly ended her romance with Wills because she didn't approve of his "roving eye." She reportedly was also concerned about the distance between them when William moved to Scotland to attend St. Andrews University.

Emma Parker Bowles: William was spotted kissing Emma at a party in 2007. The niece of Camilla Parker Bowles told reporters, "Nothing much came of it."

A FLAIR FOR FASHION

American fashion designer Michael Kors is known for dressing celebrities ranging from Jennifer Lopez and Catherine Zeta-Jones to Heidi Klum and First Lady Michelle Obama. Kors prides himself on producing clothing that looks great but is easy to wear. He believes Kate Middleton shares the same eye for effortless style.

"When I look at Kate I see a changing of the guard in what is considered elegant," he told Vogue.com. "She likes to look easy but chic. I would liken her to Obama and (French First Lady) Carla Bruni in that way. All these women are in situations where they shaking off the formal suits of their predecessors."

Kate, who first caught William's eye while modeling a see-through dress in a charity fashion show, has shown she has what it takes to become a fashion style setter. Her look is sophisticated, chic, restrained and classic. She loves wrap-style dresses, blue jeans with riding boots, and blazers in tweed or velvet.

Kate wore a simple wrap dress by Issa London when she and William stood before the media, announcing their engagement. The London-based fashion label has long been a favorite of the princess-in-training.

"It makes me very happy she wears our clothes. She's a very beautiful girl," Issa designer Daniella Issa Helayel has said.

Kate has also done wonders for the hat industry in Great Britain. She has taken to wearing what's known as a "fascinator," a wispy mini hat that is both ladylike and polished.

Of course, praise is not heaped on every look Kate dons. In January 2011, critics were quick to suggest a future princess should 1) not wear black to a wedding, and 2) not wear a top so shear (even if it's under a jacket) that tabloid reporters begin to speculate on whether she's bra-less.

Even the fashion forward can occasionally take a step backward.

"Carole and Michael are a couple whose only crime has been to start their own business and do well for themselves and their children." – A Family Friend

across the board."

The pretty, shy brunette had many friends but few boyfriends. It's long been rumored she decorated her Marlborough dorm room with a poster of the young Prince William.

"He wishes," she said in a 2010 TV interview. "No, I had the Levi's guy on my wall, not a picture of William – sorry."

After two As and a B in her final exams at school, Kate took much of 2001 as her "gap year" between studies traveling to Italy and South America. In Chile, she actually ended up working on a project Prince William had visited a month earlier.

At the end of her gap year, she moved to Scotland and enrolled at the University of St. Andrews, where she very famously met her Prince.

Kate studied art history in college and lived a life that was, by most reports, squeaky clean (beyond an occasional mooning out the window toward passing boys). After graduating in 2005, it was rumored that she planned to start her own mail-order company selling high-end children's clothes. When financing fell through, she put that plan on hold and accepted a position as an accessories buyer assistant with Jigsaw, a British clothing chain owned by family friends. She worked for Jigsaw for one year, from November 2006 to November 2007.

Kate has worked for her family's business, Party Pieces, since late 2007, a position that has allowed her the flexibility to travel with William.

As thrilled as many people are that William has found his Princess, other Royal watchers have been critical of Kate's very un-royal roots. Her mother, Carole, in particular, has been criticized in the media for everything from chewing gum at one of William's military ceremonies to ambitiously sending Kate to St. Andrews solely to meet and marry the Prince.

The Middletons have lived in Bucklebury, Berks, for 30 years and have become familiar faces at local shops and pubs. Their neighbors and friends are quick to defend the family's character and motives.

"Carole and Michael are a couple whose only crime has been to start their own business and do well for themselves and their children," a long-standing friend told The (London) Telegraph in 2010. "The fact that they raised a daughter who won the heart of Prince William should be to their credit, but I'm afraid that a lot of people are still obsessed by class in this country, and some of them will never forgive the Middletons for being middle-class."

Common by blood, Kate Middleton has proven she is, in fact, uncommonly lucky in love.

TOUR TIME

Visitors to Hollywood know they can, for around $50, hop on a bus and be driven past the homes of stars such as Leonardo DiCaprio, Brittany Spears and John Travolta.

Now, visitors to Great Britain can take similarly styled tours. The sights you'll see? Locations that helped "define the next royal golden couple."

For 15 pounds or around $15 U.S., the Royal Wedding Walk takes visitors on a two-and-a-half walking hour tour of London. Stop-off points include crown

Kate's great-grandfather; Mahiki, one of William and Kate's favorite nightclubs; and a branch of Jigsaw, the apparel and accessories retailer for whom Kate worked.

Tour organizer James Bonney told The Mirror: "It's got the potential to go crazy."

Similarly, beginning in January 2011, tour company operator Adrian Morton is sending bus tours to Bucklebury, where Middleton was raised, some 55 miles west of London.

The tour takes visitors past spots including the Old Boot Inn, Bladebone Pub & Restaurant, and the Middleton family home, which Morton admits is difficult to see because it's on a private drive obscured by trees.

Morton says Americans, in particular, seem transfixed by the young royal couple.

"There seems to be more interest in the States than in

jeweler Garrard's, who made Princess Di's engagement ring which Kate now wears; Westminster Abbey, where the couple will marry; Clarence House, scene of the press conference following the official engagement announcement; the offices of

our own country," he told The Associated Press. "I've been contacted by an American tour operator about possible tours. You can see the places where she went to school and where she was christened. And locals are interested too."

CHAPTER THREE:

Falling in Love

CHAPTER THREE: Falling in Love

Who would have thought painters Henri Matisse and Paul Cezanne would play a role in the royal romance? But they did. Sort of.

It was while Prince William and Kate Middleton were studying art history at Scotland's St. Andrews University that the two first met in 2001. Willliam eventually changed his major to geography, but not before he befriended the pretty, athletic brunette who is five months his senior.

In 2002, William and Kate moved into a four-bedroom student house along with two other friends. That's also the year that he famously paid $315 to watch Kate model a see-through black dress over a black bra and bikini bottoms in a charity fashion show.

In 2003, the duo lived with friends in a cottage on a farm outside town; they were good friends – but not boyfriend and girlfriend. In fact, Kate was dating another student, Rupert Finch, at the time and William was romantically involved with Jessica "Jecca" Craig.

Over time, William and Kate's

> *"They were very good friends for a long time and I think that blossomed into something more." – Jules Knight, friend of the royal couple*

relationship evolved from friendship to love. Kate spent several holidays with William and was among the close friends invited to his 21st birthday celebration in June 2003. The two reportedly spent weekends alone together in a cottage on the Queen's Scottish estate at Balmoral.

The St. Andrews University community was proudly protective of Prince William's privacy and allowed the love affair to unfold in relative normalcy.

"We gave them four years of normal life, four years in which they could get to know one another free of the intrusion, glare, publicity," Brian Lang, former St. Andrews principal told ABC News.

A close friend of the couple, Jules Knight, recalled William being attracted to Kate from the very beginning.

"I think he, he just took a shine to her, really," Knight told BBC America. "They spent a lot of time together and they were very good friends for a long time and I think that blossomed into something more."

While in college, Kate waited tables at a local restaurant and often met up with William after work.

"She didn't seem to be trying too hard, she wasn't, you know, dressing to the nines," pub owner Justin Hughes told ABC News. "She was just a normal girl who got on well with her boyfriend."

In March 2004, the couple enjoyed a skiing holiday in the Swiss village of Klosters. It was during this trip that they were photographed together and their romance was first exposed. Tabloid speculation about the pair went wild; William tried to dampen

THE ROYAL ROMANCE TIMELINE

April 29, 2011 – The couple exchanges marriage vows at Westminster Abbey.

Nov. 16, 2010 – The couple's engagement is officially announced.

Nov. 1, 2010 – Kate's parents are invited to join members of the royal family for a shooting holiday at Balmoral – the Queen's estate in Scotland. This is viewed as another milestone along Kate's road to acceptance by the Royal Family.

October 2010 – While on a vacation to Kenya, William asks Kate to marry him. They agree to keep their engagement secret until an official announcement can be made.

February 2010 – When asked about the prospect of a wedding, William tells the media: "You'll have to wait a while yet."

January 2010 – Kate attends William's helicopter training graduation ceremony and beams when he receives his flying badge from his father, the Prince of Wales.

April 2008 – Kate attends William's graduation from the Royal Air Force.

April 2007 – The media reports – and the Royal Family does not deny – that the couple's relationship is over. Within weeks, the same newspapers were reporting that the two were back together.

December 2006 – Kate is in the audience when William graduates from Sandhurst Military College as an Army officer.

January 2006 – The couple is photographed kissing during a vacation to the Alpine village of Klosters.

July 2005 – William and Kate enjoy a holiday at a Kenyan game reserve.

March 2004 – The couple's budding romance is made public when they are photographed on a Swiss ski vacation.

Christmas 2003 – The media is abuzz with rumors about the Prince's possible new romance.

March 2002 – Kate catches William's eye when she models a sheer black lace dress in a charity fashion show.

September 2001 – Prince William and Kate Middleton meet as students at Scotland's St. Andrews University.

WHEN WILLIAM MET KATE

Founded in 1413, St. Andrews is Scotland's oldest university and the third oldest in the English-speaking world.

The University is one of the top-rated in Europe for research, teaching quality, and student satisfaction. Recent rankings place it among the Top 20 Arts and Humanities universities in the world. Its international reputation makes it one of the most sought after destinations for prospective students from the United Kingdom, Europe, and overseas. It is Scotland's most cosmopolitan university – a third of the student body of 7,200 is from overseas.

Physically, the university is closely integrated with the coastal town of St. Andrews. On average one out of three people you see in the street have something to do with the university – ei-

ther attending classes or working there.

Of course, William and Kate aren't the first couple to find love on the St. Andrews campus. The university's press office released this statement shortly after the royal engagement was announced:

"St. Andrews is a special place – one in 10 of our students meet their future partner here, and our title as Britain's top match-making university signifies so much that is good about this community."

The St. Andrews campus is home to a beautiful chapel called St. Salvator's. The building, with its world-class pipe organ, would have been an appropriate place for William and Kate to exchange their marriage vows – if only their ceremony were less regal.

In 2006, the Woolworths retail chain commissioned "William and Kate" memorabilia in anticipation of the Royal engagement. They were a tad premature.

the frenzy by telling reporters: "I don't want to get married until I'm at least 28 or maybe 30."

William and Kate both graduated from St. Andrews in June 2005. Many royal watchers and even some friends doubted the couple would stay together once they left campus. Kate, after all, was going to work in the fashion industry in London and William was beginning his training 32 miles away at Sandhurst Military Academy. The distance proved a strain, but the couple withstood it.

In January 2006, the relationship heated up and photos of William kissing Kate in public during a ski holiday were published for the first time.

Kate was in the audience in 2006, when William was commissioned as a British Army officer. It was her first high-profile event with the Royal Family and public speculation about an impending royal wedding intensified. The retail chain Woolworths went so far as to commission T-shirts, mugs, plates, and other "William and

Kate" memorabilia.

Now planted firmly in the public eye, Kate quickly became one of the most photographed women in London. The paparazzi snapped photos – and newspapers ran them – of Kate going to work, going out with friends, taking out the garbage, even getting a parking ticket.

Gentlemanly William insisted his girlfriend should not be hounded by the media like his mother was. He asked paparazzi to leave her alone. In 2007, Kate herself filed a harassment complaint against *The Daily Mirror*. Newspaper editors admitted their reporting error and issued an apology that Kate accepted.

In 2007 the media reported that William and Kate had called it quits. Many speculated she was fed up with all the media attention. Others suggested the physical distance between them had strained the relationship. Still others insisted the Royal Family told William to dump her because Kate didn't have what it took to become a Royal bride.

The ink was barely dry on all the articles about their breakup when the same publications began reporting that William and Kate were back together. They were photographed leaving a nightclub together and again at a hunting expedition. Then, Kate sat three rows behind William in the Royal Box at London's Wembley Stadium for the Concert for Diana, a tribute event in honor of William's mother. The two didn't socialize with each other, but a source told Britain's *The Sun* newspaper at the time: "Kate and William are still working things through and insist they are not back

CHAPTER THREE: Falling in Love

public event signaled their relationship had the seal of approval from the Queen and other senior royals.

As William's military training continued, the two saw each other primarily on weekends. He became a frequent visitor to her family's home in Bucklebury and she joined him on holidays to the Caribbean, the Indian Ocean islands of the Seycelles, and skiing in Klosters.

together. But the cat is out of the bag."

Kate-watch was back on and it didn't take the keenest spy to catch Prince William visiting her at her parents' home in April 2008 – that's because he landed a Chinook helicopter from the Royal Air Force fleet in their yard. William also flew a Chinook – without permission – to a friend's bachelor party on the Isle of Wight, the largest island of England, located in the English Channel. Military officials confirmed the incidents.

Unauthorized helicopter use withstanding, William graduated from his first flying course in Spring 2008 and, when he did, Kate was in the audience. Her presence at such an important and

Kate and William began sharing a cottage on the Welsh island of Anglesey in early 2010, near the Royal Air Force base where the prince is based. A few months later, the pair made a public showing of their commitment to each other by officially announcing their engagement.

While thousands of young women wish they were so lucky as to marry a prince, a poised and confident Kate reportedly told friends in 2007: "He's lucky to be going out with me!"

And now, they both agree, he's lucky to be marrying her.

LOVE WAS IN THE STARS

It may have taken eight years of on-again, off-again dating for Prince William to come to the conclusion that Kate was "the one" but according to astrologers love was always in the stars.

William's June 21 birthday makes him a Cancer. Kate's January 9 birth-date makes her a Capricorn. Astrologically speaking, experts say the two couldn't be more compatible.

"It's kind of like two halves of an apple coming together," astrologer Susan Miller, founder of astrology-zone.com, told the *CBS Early Show*. "They're so perfect together, it`s crazy. And her moon is in Cancer, his moon is in Cancer. There's a coming together. There's a feeling of safety and security between these two."

As a Cancer, Miller says one of William's key qualities is that he's very family-oriented, which should serve him well both as a husband and as the future king.

"In a sense, he is taking over the family business," she said. "He's intuitive, emotional, and that's nice in a man. You know, his feelings come right up to the surface. She'll always know what he's feeling."

According to her astrological sign, Kate is a born leader. Capricorns are known for their down-to-earth nature, practicality, ambitiousness, and patience.

Additionally, Kate was born on the day of a full moon and a lunar eclipse. According to the website astrology-room.com, those born on an eclipse tend to have a life directed by the forces of destiny. For Kate, it appears destiny has led her toward a relationship that is changing her life in the most dramatic of ways.

Astrologyzone.com's Miller says many people end up marrying someone who has the same astrological sign as one of their parents, which aids in compatibility. Not only is William the

To commemorate the wedding of Prince William to Kate Middleton 29th April 2011

same sign as Kate's father, Michael Middleton, but their birthdays are just two days apart: William's is June 21 and Mr. Middleton's is June 23.

"This is perfect, perfect, perfect," said Miller. "I would say that there are many, many, many favorable things about this pairing. I think this is an exciting pairing and he's going to make a great husband."

The Royal Engagement

CHAPTER FOUR: The Royal Engagement

An eight-year, on-again, off-again courtship with Prince William had earned Kate Middleton the nickname "Waity Katy."

On November 16, 2010, her wait was finally over.

That's the day Prince Charles' Clarence House office proclaimed that the heir to the British throne was "delighted to announce the engagement of Prince William to Miss Catherine Middleton."

"It was only right the two were put together." — Prince William speaking of his mother's engagement ring and his new fiancé.

Looking joyful and very much in love, the couple stood before flashing cameras as they announced their engagement at St. James Palace, the oldest palace of the Sovereign, which is often used for official Royal functions.

After the news had been announced, the two shared a bit of insight into their relationship. Kate wore the brilliant blue sapphire and diamond engagement ring that the Prince's father gave to Princess Diana in 1981.

"Well, as you may recognize now, it's my mother's engagement ring and it's very special to me, as Kate is very special to me now as well," Prince William said. "It was only right the two were put together. It was my way of making sure mother didn't miss out on today and the excitement and the fact that we're going to spend the rest of our lives together."

With her arm threaded through his, Kate called the prince a "loving boyfriend," gently teased him about his cooking skills, and recalled how he'd been "very supportive of me in good times and also through the bad times."

Prince William said of the engagement: "The timing is right now, we are both very, very happy. We both have a very good sense of humor and we take the mickey out of each other (tease each other) a lot."

The Prince told reporters he had asked Kate to marry him during a private October 2010 vacation to Kenya. At the time, they were visiting the remote Rotundu Log Cabins complex on Mount Kenya.

William told Britain's ITV News he'd been carrying the ring in his rucksack for about three weeks before the proposal.

"Everywhere I went, I was keeping a hold of it 'cause I knew if this thing disappeared, I'd be in a lot of trouble," he said.

Despite years of public speculation about when the couple would wed, Kate said the proposal came as a total surprise to her.

"He's a true romantic, and we had a wonderful holiday in Africa, and it was out there in a very quiet lodge and it was very romantic and very personal time for both of us," she said. "We were out there with friends, so I really didn't expect it at all. It was a total shock when it came."

In a television interview, William admitted he asked Kate to marry him

WHAT IS CLARENCE HOUSE?

Most official announcements about the Royal Family are made by the staff of Clarence House, the official residence of Charles, The Prince of Wales, and Camilla, The Duchess of Cornwall. In addition to living quarters, Clarence House also provides office space for The Royal Highnesses' official staff to support them in undertaking their public and charitable duties.

Clarence House stands beside St James's Palace in downtown London. It was built between 1825 and 1827; the four-story building was renovated and redecorated from 2002 to 2003.

These days, the Prince and Duchess receive official guests at Clarence House, routinely hosting official lunches, receptions, and dinners. Several thousand are received at the House annually.

Clarence House is open to the public between August and October each year. Visitors are given a guided tour of the five ground-floor rooms, where they are able to see items from the Royal Collection and from the collection of Queen Elizabeth, the Queen Mother. The Queen Mother's collection is particularly strong in 20th Century British art, with important works by John Piper, Graham Sutherland, W. S. Sickert, and Augustus John.

ROYAL COLLECTIBLES

Souvenir-makers launched into action even before William and Kate officially announced their engagement, mindful that memorabilia of Charles and Diana's 1981 nuptials are still highly sought by collectors.

Experts estimate the 2011 wedding could boost the struggling British economy by the equivalency of more than $900 million through sales of merchandise and tourism.

Almost as soon as the Royal engagement was announced, souvenir shops and chinaware producers were inundated with order requests for special edition mugs,

plates, and assorted collectibles.

The Alderney coin, inspired by photos of the couple at a sporting event, has the Queen's seal of approval and is being produced by the Royal Mint. The Royal Mint has issued other medals and coins to honor the British monarchy for more than 1,100 years, but this is the first engagement design it has produced.

The desire for William and Kate memorabilia comes from around the globe. Interest in the United States, where the Royal family is viewed with a sort of wonder, is high. For Brits – especially those living abroad – owning royal collectibles is a way to connect with their country.

"For the British, it's a feeling of security," Stephen Church, whose family sells collectibles from a shop in England's Northampton, told *The Christian Science Monitor*. "It's part of life's routine that the royal family is there. Buying commemorative products is part of cherishing them."

William and Kate's images are decorating items ranging from T-shirts and thimbles to key rings and cell phone covers.

Church explains that Royal births, coronations, and weddings have been marked with souvenir china and ceramics for centuries. Most serious collectors, he says, will skip the Royal tape dispensers and swimsuit cover-ups in favor of plates and tea cups.

It is predicted demand also will be high for high-end items including hand-painted enamel boxes, loving cups (styles with two handles), and heart-shaped China trays.

One company, Royal Crown Derby, is selling white and gold swan paperweights (called William and Catherine) with necks curved to form a heart. And, for those who already have their fill of wedding collectibles, company representatives say they're already working of designs to celebrate much-anticipated Royal babies.

before asking her father for permission.

"I was torn between asking Kate's dad first and then the realization he might actually say no," the Prince told Britain's ITV. "I thought, if I ask Kate first, then he can't really say no, so I did it that way round and managed to speak to Mike sort of soon after."

When asked by reporters why it took him so long to propose, a blushing William responded, "I also didn't realize it was a race, otherwise I probably would've been a lot quicker."

Prince William made a point of telling reporters that, although Kate wears his mother's ring, she is in no way standing in her shadow.

"There's no pressure," he said. "No one is trying to fill my mother's shoes. What she did was fantastic. It's about making your own future and your own destiny, and Kate will do a very good job of that."

Well wishes for the young couple started streaming in even before their short announcement ceremony at St. James Palace had ended.

William's younger brother, Prince Harry, chimed in with an official statement that read: "I am delighted that my brother popped the question. It means I get a sister, which I have always wanted."

As soon as the engagement was announced in London, Kate's father, Michael Middleton, read a statement on behalf of her parents outside their home near the Berkshire village of Buckleberry:

"Carole and I are absolutely delighted by today's announcement and thrilled at the prospect of a wedding some time next year. As you know, Catherine and Prince William have been going out for quite a number of years which has been great for us because we have got to know William very well. We all think he is wonderful and we are extremely fond of him. They make a lovely couple, they are great fun to be with,

> *"I was torn between asking Kate's dad first and then the realization he might actually say no." – Prince William in regard to seeking the Middletons' permission to propose*

and we've had a lot of laughs together. We wish them every happiness for the future."

As a sign of the times, the engagement was also officially announced on Facebook and Twitter. Within just 25 minutes of the announcement's post on the Royal Facebook page, nearly 1,500 people had indicated they "liked" the news. The Monarch's Twitter feed heralded the news with a tweet:

@BritishMonarchy The Queen and The Duke of Edinburgh are absolutely delighted at the news of Prince William and Catherine Middleton's engagement.

Similarly, Prince Charles also tweeted his joy:

READY TO TAKE AN "ENGAGEMENTCATION"?

It used to be that a fancy restaurant or a secluded beach could provide the perfect place for a young man to get down on one knee and ask his beloved to marry him. Now, it appears Prince William has upped the ante.

His Royal Highness took longtime gal pal Kate on a trip to Kenya to propose. And that was all it took to start a new trend known as "engagementcations" – vacations dedicated to getting engaged.

According to American Express travel specialists, the most requested amenity for romance travel isn't champagne, heart-shaped bathtubs, or rose petals to sprinkle on the bed, but rather location recommendations for marriage proposals.

Honeymoons are Forever, a boutique travel company based in Salinas, Calif., cautions that an engagementcation takes a little more planning that your average vacation. The company's travel experts offer these tips to help you pull off a Prince William-esque engagement vacation:

- Choose a destination that has meaning for you as a couple. This might not be the best time to go somewhere for the first time, especially if your intended hasn't mentioned wanting to visit your chosen location.

- If your beloved is a private person, make the engagement private. Conversely, if your bride-to-be is an extrovert, you might think about putting your proposal up in lights at the ballpark or having it written across the sky.

- Safeguard the ring. If you're going on a river-rafting excursion down the Colorado River, you might want to consider a "faux ring" to propose with, leaving the sparkler at home.

- Work with your vacation planner to arrange a stealthy photographer to capture your special event.

- Consider proposing early in the vacation. Once the big question has been asked – and answered – you'll be able to relax and enjoy the rest of your trip.

CHAPTER FOUR: The Royal Engagement

As a sign of the times, the royal engagement was announced via Twitter and on Facebook where, within 25 minutes, nearly 1,500 people indicated they "liked" the news.

@ClarenceHouse The Prince of Wales is delighted to announce the engagement of Prince William to Miss Catherine Middleton.

Prince Charles was in Dorset when the announcement was issued. He told reporters he was "thrilled" and joked that the couple had been "practicing long enough."

United Kingdom Prime Minister David Cameron was told of the engagement during a Cabinet meeting and immediately shared the news with his cabinet. Emerging from a meeting that morning, he told members of the press: "I spoke to Prince William a few moments ago and passed on my congratulations. He was obviously extremely excited about the news and thrilled about what lies in store. It was wonderful to have that word with him and pass along my best wishes. This is incredibly exciting news and I am sure the whole country will want to pass on their congratulations."

Of course, dignitaries weren't the only ones thrilled to hear about the engagement. Royal-watchers quickly snatched up newspapers, huddled around televisions, and jumped online in hopes of learning every romantic detail about the affair. In fact, in a one-hour span in the middle of the day on November 16, 2010 – the day of the official announcement – 45,000 different news stories were indexed through Google News containing the phrase "Prince William."

The wait was over. The people's Prince was engaged. This was good cause for celebration.

ROYAL CABINS?

Forget glitz and glamour. When Prince William proposed to the lovely Kate Middleton, he did so in one of the most remote places on earth.

The Prince reportedly got engaged October 20, 2010, at Rutundu Log Cabins, located on the northern slopes of Mount Kenya, 10,200 feet above sea-level. The cabins are situated just above the forest line, overlooking Lake Rutundu, which is privately stocked with rainbow trout.

The cabins, described as "rustic chic," are marketed as the "perfect escape from the 'safari circuit' or the bustle of Nairobi."

The accommodations are built in original log cabin style with moss filling the gaps between logs and the roof. Furnished with four-poster beds constructed from local lumber and sheepskin rugs, the cabins – there are two – have fireplaces and en-suite bathrooms with flush toilets. There is no electricity, but the cabins are a favorite spot of the prince due to their privacy. Rental rates for the cabins average $167 per person per night.

Both William and Kate signed the cabin's visitor's book. Kate – who signed her full name, Catherine Middleton – wrote: "Thank you for such a wonderful 24 hours! Sadly no fish to be found but we had great fun trying. I love the warm fires and candle lights - so romantic! Hope to be back again soon." William added: "Such fun to be back! Brought more clothes this time! Looked after so well. Thank you guys! Look forward to next time, soon I hope."

The couple reportedly drove to Rutundu from Lewa Downs, the Kenyan wildlife reserve where they have vacationed in the past and where Prince William spent part of his gap year before attending the University of St. Andrews.

"I think Kenya has always been very close to Prince William's heart," Ian Craig, founder of the Lewa Wildlife Conservancy, told CNN. "He's been coming here for many years. He loves it. I think he wanted to share Kenya with his new bride, unknown to us at the time."

Comparisons to Charles and Di

CHAPTER FIVE: Comparisons to Charles and Di

million people stood in the streets on that gray day – tens of thousands of them having camped out overnight to claim their spots along the processional route – to catch a glimpse of the Royal couple. King Olav V of Norway, King Baudouin and Queen Fabiola of Belgium, Queen Margrethe II and Prince Henrik of Denmark,

and U.S. First Lady Nancy Reagan were among 3,500 who witnessed the ceremony inside St. Paul's; another 750 million people worldwide tuned in to watch the wedding on television.

The smaller, less-grandiose-but-hardly-shabby Westminster Abbey will be the location of William and Kate's wedding. Their guest list for the ceremony is expected to include 2,000 people, many of them world leaders and dignitaries. It's predicted

as many as 1 billion people will tune in to watch the ceremony on television; many more are likely to catch Internet feeds or listen on the radio.

Diana, then 20 years old, traveled to her 11:20 a.m. wedding from Clarence House in a Cinderella-esque glass coach.

Kate, 29, will be the oldest woman ever to marry a future King of England. She's opted to break with tradition and travel to her 11 a.m. nuptials by car. The couple will leave Westminster Abbey in a Royal coach.

"It's symbolic," Royals biographer Kitty Kelley told *USA Today*, pointing to Kate's middle-class roots. "If she got into a royal coach going to the Abbey, everyone would go crazy, but if she's married to a future king when she gets into it, then it will be all right."

Diana was given in marriage by her father, the eighth Earl Spencer, a friend of the Royal Family since birth. Kate will be given in her marriage by her non-royal father, Michael Middleton, a former airline worker who now owns a party goods business.

During the 1981 ceremony, both the bride and groom let jitters get the best of them, misspeaking slightly as they exchanged vows. Diana inverted the Prince's names, calling him "Philip Charles Arthur George." Charles reportedly joked to his

DIANA'S DRESS

The details of Diana's wedding gown were kept secret until the moment she stepped out of the glass carriage at St. Paul's. That's when the entire world let out a collective gasp of admiration.

Designed by David and Elizabeth Emanuel, the gown had huge, puffed sleeves and frilly neckline. Adorned with lace, hand embroidery, sequins and 10,000 pearls, the dress had a 25-foot-long train.

Most of the materials used in the dress were made in Britain. The Emanuels and their team constructed the gown from three different fabrics, including high-quality taffeta made from silk woven on Britain's Lullingstone silk farm, 100 yards of tulle, and lace that once belong to Queen Mary.

"The romantic ruffle that the Princess of Wales has made her fashion hallmark was the focal point of her fairytale wedding dress," wrote Suzy Menkes of the *London Times*. "The impression given as she stepped from her glass coach, with a full skirt below a tiny waist and the shimmering train snaking behind her, was of freshness and romance."

Menkes, who has a reputation as one of the fashion world's toughest critics, called the dress "a triumph both in its overall conception and in its tiniest detail."

Among those tiny details were Diana's silk slippers, which barely peaked out from under her full skirt. The heart-shaped central motif on each of the slippers was decorated with 150 pearls and 500 sequins.

The gown's designers wrote a book called *A Dress for Diana*, in which they described the process of designing the gown. They said they strived to balance the fact that she was a young woman who wanted a feminine dress with the need to make a gown dramatic enough for someone who was about to become the Princess of Wales.

The gown had an immediate and widespread effect on the bridal market. According to Associated Press reports, the first copy of the dress appeared in the window of a shop on London's Oxford Street just five hours after the ceremony. The knock-off was created by Ellis Bridals, whose seamstresses got to work the instant they saw Diana leave Clarence House.

CAMILLA BECOMES A DUCHESS

Prince Charles married Camilla Parker Bowles on April 9, 2005, in a small, private wedding at Windsor's Guildhall. Afterward, about 800 family members and friends attended a service of blessing at Windsor Castle. Following their union, Camilla became Duchess of Cornwall.

The couple's wedding originally was set for April 8, 2005, at Windsor Castle. In order to host a civil marriage ceremony, Windsor Castle would have to get a license; a condition of such a license is that the venue must be available for a period of one year to anyone wishing to be married there. The Royal Family didn't want Windsor Castle available to the public for civil marriages, so the location had to be changed.

Then, on April 4, it was announced that the wedding would be delayed by one day to allow the Prince of Wales and some of the invited dignitaries to attend the funeral of Pope John Paul II.

Although 20,000 well-wishers gathered at Windsor's Guildhall to cheer the newlyweds, several of their own family members chose to skip the affair. Charles' parents and Camilla's father did not attend. Queen Elizabeth II and the Duke of Edinburgh did, however, attend the service of blessing and held a reception for the couple at Windsor Castle.

Following the wedding, the couple traveled to the Prince's country home in Scotland for their honeymoon.

The wedding brought to a conclusion a relationship that began 35 years earlier, when the two met at a polo match in 1970. They began good friends but went their own ways romantically. Camilla married cavalry officer Andrew Parker Bowles in 1973; they divorced in 1995. Charles married Diana Spencer in 1981; they separated in 1992 and divorced in 1996.

Camilla was Charles' mistress during his marriage to Diana, a fact which was whispered about for many years but was not confirmed until the 1990s.

CHAPTER FIVE: Comparisons to Charles and Di

bride: "Diana, you have actually married my father."

Charles promised "with all thy goods I share with thee" instead of "all my worldly goods I share with thee."

While professing your love and loyalty in front of a billion-plus people is enough to shake just about anyone's nerves, Kate has already proven she's calmer and more confident than young Diana was when she married her Prince.

Diana's dress was a puff ball meringue wedding gown, with huge puffed sleeves and a frilly neckline. She wore an elaborate diamond and silver Spencer family tiara which, she later revealed, gave her a splitting headache.

While details surrounding Kate's wedding day attire remain a closely guarded secret until the big day, Deborah Joseph, editor of *Brides Magazine,* said the new bride was under substantial pressure to choose an English designer. Joseph and other fashion pros expected Kate would choose a soft fabric, like tulle or organza, in favor of the stiff taffeta Diana used.

Diana's wedding gown designer, Elizabeth Emanuel, hoped Kate would keep her dress simple.

"I think she's got a very good figure, so she should probably wear something quite simple, but with a really nice, strong silhouette," Emanuel told TooFab.com. "Probably classic, but with a bit of an edge to it, since she's got a good fashion sense.

Following their wedding, Charles and

Diana traveled to Buckingham Palace where they appeared on the balcony. The couple delighted well-wishers by waving

and kissing – a tradition William and Kate are likely to follow.

While the differences between 1981 and 2011 Royal wedding fabrics, transportation, and guest lists are likely to be critiqued for years to come, the thing most Royal-watchers agree on now is that Kate is not Diana. Sure, she may be walking the fine line between showing the proper respect to William's late mother and living life in her shadow, but it's a line she's – so far – been able to toe.

At the official press event announcing their engagement, Kate told reporters

she viewed the late Royal as an "inspirational" figure.

"Obviously, I would have loved to have met her and she's obviously an inspirational woman to look up to," she told reporters. "On this day and going forward and things, you know, it is a wonderful family, the members who I've met have achieved a lot and (are) very inspirational."

London Daily Mail reporter Sarah Sands wrote a column about the many differences between Diana and Kate, one of the most notable being their familiarity with the men with whom they pledged to share their lives.

"Diana, with all her sweetness and complexity, wedded a man whom she did not really know," Sands wrote. "Kate has lived with William for years, knowing him first as a friend and fellow undergraduate at St. Andrews University, and then as a girlfriend. … Kate has reportedly been welcomed by the Firm, who have modernized their expectation of marriage …"

Cosima Somerset, a one-time confidante of Diana, has told the media about her conversations, many of which focused on the late Princess' concern for her sons. Diana, said Somerset, was proud of the boys' curiosity, protective of their privacy, and concerned about their futures.

It's a sure bet she'd have found comfort in knowing William would one day fall in love with a modern-day, albeit more confident, version of herself.

WHAT ABOUT ANDREW & SARAH?

Prince Andrew – Charles' younger brother – is the second son of Queen Elizabeth II and Prince Philip, Duke of Edinburgh. He married Sarah Ferguson in 1986 at Westminster Abbey. They became known as the Duke and Duchess of York.

Many comparisons have been made between the weddings of Prince Charles and Prince William – likely because they are father and son, and because Charles and William are first and second in line

Courtesy of AP Images

to the throne. It's possible, too, that mentions of Andrew's wedding are fewer because many Brits are deeply embarrassed by the actions of his now ex-wife.

Andrew and Sarah's wedding was grand in every aspect. She arrived from Clarence House in a Glass Coach. Her walk up the Abbey aisle took four minutes, the bride's 17-foot train trailing behind. Inside the church, 2,000 people watched the ceremony; outside after the wedding, 100,000 people gathered to see their first

public kiss as husband and wife on the balcony of the Buckingham Palace.

The couple had two daughters, Princess Beatrice in 1988 and Princes Eugenie in 1990. They divorced in 1996 but reunited briefly after that for the sake of their girls. In a 2001 interview with an American magazine, Sarah said her marriage began to disintegrate within a week of the wedding. She blamed Prince Andrew's naval duties.

Following the divorce, Sarah was saddled with debt and earned a good deal of money as TV spokeswoman for the Weight Watchers diet program. She also published several children's books about Budgie the Helicopter. In 1992 – while she was still married to the Prince – photos emerged of the duchess on vacation with U.S. oil tycoon Steve Wyatt. Months later she was photographed topless while having her toes sucked by John Bryan, her financial adviser. In 2010, the drunken former duchess was caught on camera by the British tabloid *News of the World*, selling a rich businessman access to her ex-husband, who now works as a trade envoy for the British government.

The late Lord Charteris, one of the Queen's senior courtiers, referred to Sarah Ferguson in the 1990s as: "Vulgar, vulgar, vulgar." He was not alone in his assessment which, perhaps, is why Andrew's fairytale wedding to the once-beaming redhead is rarely discussed in royal circles.

CHAPTER SIX:

The Wedding and Beyond

CHAPTER SIX: The Wedding and Beyond

There's nothing like the announcement of a royal wedding to get speculation flowing – on just about everything. Where would the wedding take place? Who would be invited? What would the wedding dress look like? William and Kate, through Clarence House, released the nitty-gritty details piecemeal:

- On Nov. 23, 2010, it was announced the wedding would take place beginning at 11 a.m. on April 29, 2011.

- On Jan. 5, 2011, the couple shared that they planned to travel via carriage from their wedding ceremony along the Royals' traditional processional route.
- Nine days later, on Jan. 16, 2011, it was announced that, instead of buying gifts, wedding guests would be asked to donate to the couple's selected charities.

While many Royal-watchers assumed the gradual sharing of details was designed to torture them, the truth is – even with a full staff to help – wedding planning takes time. The tiniest decisions become monstrous when you realize they'll be played out on a world stage. And making those decisions requires research that must be carried out under a cloak of secrecy if there's any hope of, say, wearing a dress that hasn't already been seen by 6.8 billion people.

The ceremony is expected to fall between the lavish spectacle of Charles and Di's 1981 nuptials and Charles' private wedding to Camilla, Duchess of Cornwall, in 2005.

In fact, officials at Buckingham Palace and St. James Palace say William and Kate's wedding will, in many ways, be more of an echo of the wedding of his grandparents than that of his parents. The marriage of then-Princess Elizabeth to the Duke of Edinburgh was cause for national celebration, but it took place in 1947 when Britain was

struggling to recover from the economic impact of World War II.

"Let's face it, many people would be disappointed if William and Kate were to get married in private and we never even caught a glimpse of Kate's dress, as has become the trend with A-list celebrities," *Cosmopolitan Bride* editor Miranda Eason told the (Bristol) *Western Daily Press.* "For an heir to the throne to have a big wedding is almost part of the job description."

Prince William's private secretary, Jamie Lowther-Pinkerton, said William and Kate were striving to plan a wedding that was "a proper celebration for the nation and the realms." At the same time, he said, they were "very mindful" of striking the right balance given the strained economic times.

"It will be done properly and well, but not in an ostentatious and lavish manner," one courtier told the BBC in January 2011.

Clarence House announced early on that Kate would arrive at her Westminster Abbey wedding via car, making hers the first Royal wedding arrival since 1963 not to feature a fairy tale horse-drawn coach entrance. The gesture has been hailed both as a cost-saving measure and as a nod to modern times. Still others say it's only proper for Kate to skip the pre-wedding carriage since she's a commoner.

Another sign of budget slashing? Fewer than half the 2,000 members of the Abbey congregation will be invited to a reception hosted by the Queen. The event will feature a buffet instead of a more traditional, formal, sit-down meal.

The Royals and the Middletons planned to pay for the wedding itself, but taxpayers

Kate Middleton becomes the first bride since 1963 to arrive at her royal wedding in something other than a horse-drawn carriage. She's opting for a car.

would meet the cost of extra security, street cleaning, and transportation.

Royal weddings, after all, call for expenditures most commoners could never imagine. For example, teams of cleaners will be deployed the night before the wedding to ensure the city looks its best. Similar teams will be deployed to clear litter after the crowds have gone. London city officials say the cost of cleaning central London's streets could cost 40,000 pounds or about $63,500.

Additional policing is also costly. With the guest list including royalty and political leaders from around the world, months of preparation and monitoring of specific threats is expected to cost more than $125 million. Royal protection, special branch, armed police, diplomatic protection, and beat officers are certain to be involved.

Jenny Jones, a member of the Metropolitan Police Authority, told the London Telegraph security was of utmost importance because the wedding would present a "fantastic opportunity" for terrorists.

Those extraordinary costs have many

Thanks to merchandising and increased tourism, experts predict the Royal wedding could give the British economy a $984 million boost.

politicians and citizens calling for the Queen to pay for all wedding costs.

"The Queen's personal wealth is estimated at £290 million ($460 million)," said Jones, who is also a Green Party politician. "I just think she has got to pay for it."

"I don't even have enough money for my own wedding, let alone theirs," London construction worker Scott Northgrave told *The Economic Times*. "They have a fortune, why not use it?"

Others insist benefits to the country's economy will far outweigh the final bill.

Neil Saunders, consulting director of retail researchers Verdict, said merchandising, increased tourism to the UK, and a feel-good factor that will increase retail sales before and after the wedding could give the economy the equivalent of a $984 million consumer spending boost. Saunders said Britain's tourism industry alone could benefit by more than $320 million.

Perhaps in an effort to deflect attention from the costs of their actual ceremony, William and Kate made an announcement in the last week of 2010 regarding how they plan to keep their post-wedding household budget low: They don't plan to have any servants. They didn't have them prior to their engagement and, at least in the short term, they don't plan to have them in the

WESTMINSTER ABBEY

When William and Kate exchange marriage vows, they'll be doing so in Westminster Abbey, a church that's older than many modern countries.

Also known as the Collegiate Church of St. Peter, Westminster Abbey was founded in 960 by Benedictine monks. It has served as the official coronation and burial church of the Monarch since 1066 and holds the remains of 17 British Kings.

William and Kate's wedding will be the sixteenth royal wedding to be held at Westminster Abbey, dating back to 1100, when King Henry I married Princess Edith "Matilda." Queen Elizabeth II had both her wedding and coronation at the Abbey.

William's parents, Prince Charles and Lady Diana, did not marry at Westminster Abbey. Instead, their 3,500 guests gathered at St. Paul's Cathedral, which is considerably larger. (Westminster holds around 2,000 people.) Funeral services for Diana, Princess of Wales, were held in the Abbey in 1997.

Located next to the Houses of Parliament in the heart of London, Westminster Abbey is a Gothic-style monastery. Because of its royal connections, it was saved from the destruction King Henry VIII wrought on monastic buildings during the Reformation.

The Abbey is very much a living, breathing church, hosting more than 1,500 worship and special services each year.

Modern-day visitors to the Abbey are treated to a fascinating sampling of English history: a medieval coronation throne; a Poet's Corner with memorials to William Shakespeare, Charles Dickens, and others; and the tombs of Queen Elizabeth I, explorer David Livingstone, and naturalist Charles Darwin.

future. The news was greeted with a mix of adoration and skepticism.

"I think the image they are trying to portray is that these are new, modern, young royals who don't need a coterie of staff to help them get on with their daily lives," Roya Nikkhah, royal correspondent for the *Sunday Telegraph*, a British newspaper, told CBS News.

William's father, Prince Charles has 149 staffers – 25 of them personal servants fulfilling roles such as valets and butlers.

Similarly, at Buckingham Palace, it can take a large staff of servants up to three days just to prepare the table for a state banquet.

Some royal watchers doubt the couple will last long doing their own laundry and cleaning. Others say William was so disturbed by the ways in which past staff

ANOTHER QUEEN CATHERINE?

If Prince William becomes King, Kate will become Queen, sort of. She will be the Queen Consort, which is the official title of the spouse of the reigning King, and would be known as Queen Catherine. However, as a commoner with no direct royal lin-

eage, she would not be able to assume the throne. If anything happened to her husband, the honor would pass either directly to one of their children or to Prince Harry.

There have been five previous Queen Catherines (albeit not all spelled the same) – three of them married to Henry VIII. Here's a look at Queen Catherines of the past:

Catherine of Valois, daughter of the King of France, was married to Henry V of England in 1420. Catherine of Valois also was the mother of Henry VI and grandmother of Henry VII.

Catherine of Aragon was the first wife of King Henry VIII of England. After 24 years of marriage, during which no male heir was produced, Henry VIII moved to have the union annulled, setting into motion a chain of events that led to England's break with the Roman Catholic Church. Prior to marrying Henry VIII, Catherine was Princess of Wales, having been married to Arthur Prince of Wales.

Kathryn Howard became Henry VIII's fifth wife in 1540, when he was 49 and she was 19. The King reportedly described his new bride as his "rose without a thorn." She was beheaded in 1542 for allegedly having an affair with one of Henry's courtiers.

Katherine Parr, who had been widowed twice before, wed Henry VIII in 1542. Henry VIII died in January 1547, making Katherine a widow for a third time. Just a few months after his death, she married Thomas Seymour; the quickness and secret nature of the union caused a huge scandal.

Catherine of Braganza married King Charles II in 1662. This particular Queen Kate was Portuguese, a Catholic, and purportedly a great drinker of tea. When she first married Charles II she didn't speak English, making her a particularly unpopular queen.

members betrayed his mother and her memory that they think he'll hold out as long as he can.

Once married, William and Kate will live in North Wales, where William is based with the Royal Air Force. They'll also have use of an apartment at Clarence House, where Prince Charles and the Duchess of Cornwall and Prince Henry also have suites. When William finishes his military assignment, he and Kate are expected to move into a house built by Charles at Harewood Park in Herfordshire. The neo-Georgian house is located on a 900-acre estate in the countryside between Monmouth and Ross-in-Wye. The home, which was built to be eco-friendly, is said to include two grand reception rooms, a drawing room, six bedrooms, study, kitchen, pantry, boot room, and even a chapel.

Even as the couple was still busy picking out floral bouquets and bridesmaid dresses and long before they'd unpack boxes in their marital home, divorce experts around the world were offering unsolicited advice about pre-nuptial agreements and more.

Diana's private secretary, Patrick Jephson, told The *Daily Mail*: "There will be a tidal wave of sentimental slush, but I believe what I'm saying. You've got to be practical. If (Kate) was my sister, I'd tell her to get a good pre-nup."

Jephson, who had an insider's view of Charles and Diana's strained relationship, suggested Kate carve out a definite role for herself. "Kate's not just going into a marriage; she's going into a business."

He predicted this modern-day Royal

GREETING THE ROYALS

There are no hard and fast rules for how one should act when meeting the Queen or a member of the Royal Family.

Should you get an invitation to Prince William and Kate's wedding, you may want to observe the traditional forms, as suggested by the official website of the British Monarchy:

Men should perform a neck bow (from the head only) while women should do a small curtsy. A simple handshake is also acceptable.

When meeting the Queen, the correct initial address is "Your Majesty" and, after that, "Ma'am."

For male members of the Royal Family the same rules apply, with the title used in the first instance being "Your Royal Highness" and, subsequently, "Sir."

For other female members of the Royal Family, the first address is conventionally "Your Royal Highness" followed by "Ma'am" in later conversation.

marriage has a better chance at succeeding because Kate is older, more experienced, and more confident than Diana was when she married Charles.

"She knows William better," he told the *Daily Mail*. "If you get it right, it's the best job in the world. It can be fantastic. They should set off with the firm intention of making it the happiest job in the world."

THE RING

If William and Kate follow tradition (and let's face it, tradition is at the heart of any royal affair), her wedding ring is likely to be made from a nugget of Welsh gold.

Welsh gold has been used for royal brides' rings since 1923, when the Queen Mother started the trend. Subsequently, Welsh gold was used to make the Queen's ring in 1947,

the largest and richest of all gold mines in the Dolgellau mining area. The mine has closed and re-opened several times for small-scale operations; it most recently closed in 1998 and has not since re-opened.

Only a gram of the original nugget remains. Fortunately, in 1981, the British Royal Legion presented the Queen with a 36-gram piece of Welsh gold for future royal wedding rings. Gold from the new nugget was used to make a ring for Sarah, Duchess of York, in 1986.

In addition to her wedding ring, Kate has received a very famous engagement ring: It originally belonged to William's mother, Princess Diana.

Princess Margaret's in 1960, the Princess Royal's in 1973, Princess Diana's in 1981, and Camilla's in 2005. In fact, all those rings were made from the same nugget – a chunk of gold that came from St. David's Mine on Clogau Mountain in North Wales. The mine was once

Diana received the ring from Prince Charles after the two were engaged in 1981. At the time, the ring – which features a large sapphire surrounded by 14 diamonds – cost 30,000 pounds or about $48,000.

happiness a cape then?
G2 Page 11 Trends that die
G2 Page 14

theguard

£1.00
Wednesday 17.11.10
Published
in London and
Manchester
guardian.co.uk

A royal wedding in the age of austerity Kate and William

Prince William announced that they had become engaged on holiday in Kenya in October. They will marry next year. Photograph: Ben Stansall/AFP

THE SÜN

£9.50

lls & Kate
gagement

VENIR EDITION

With Mummy's
ring I thee wed

12-PAGE ROYAL WEDDING PULLOUT INSIDE

FINANCIAL TI

Wednesday November 17 2010 | £2.00

Sponsoring equality
Sylvia Hewlett on a woman's path to the top. Comment, Page 15

World Business Newspaper

What happe
a start-up g
Judgment call.

News Briefing

BT warns of challenge to Ofcom over fees
Ian Livingston, BT's chief, said the group could sue the telecoms regulator if it refused to allow it to repair its pension deficit partly through a rise in wholesale fees levied on rivals. Page 19 R.com/fotografias

UK stance hits Google
The UK will not find EU's should be free to favour traffic from one content provider over another as long as they tell customers – a blow to Google and to the BBC. Page 4

Bout extradited to US
Alleged weapons dealer Viktor Bout, a former Soviet air force officer who maintains his innocence, was extradited from Thailand to the US, causing an angry Russian response. Page 6

Guantánamo pay-outs
Britain will pay £10m to a dozen former inmates of Cuba's Guantánamo Bay centre in order to settle a legal case in which they claimed the UK security services were complicit in their torture. Page 1

US arms deal setback
Barack Obama's hopes of pushing through a set-piece arms control treaty with Russia

Rescue
team sets
up talks
in Dublin

UK considers billions
in loans for neighbour

Aid 'not inevitable' says
Irish finance minister

By Peter Spiegel and
Joshua Chaffin in Brussels
and George Parker in London

European Union authorities said Dublin have agreed that a team of EU and International Monetary Fund officials will visit Ireland for what senior European

summit of finance ministers from the 16 countries that use the euro.
Brian Lenihan, Ireland's finance minister, said after the meeting that it was "not inevitable" that the country would require a bail-out, but said the talks would begin this week.
"I'm not going to impose time-lines, but this is agreed," Mr Lenihan said of the new talks. "We do have to examine how security and stability can be brought into the system.

Royal union Prince William to we

WEDNESDAY, NOVEMBER 17, 2010
www.dailymail.co.uk
50p

FREE INSIDE
Superb 16-page souvenir pull-out

Daily Mail

Royal engagement 16 pages of souve

The Daily Teleg

NEWSPAPER OF THE YEAR

Wednesday, November 17, 2010

Kate's very sp

Prince's verdict on his bride-to-be – and that's why she deser

By Gordon Rayner
Chief Reporter

PRINCE William proposed to Kate Middleton with his late mother's favourite ring, to bring together the two most "special" women in his life.
After seven years of speculation, the couple announced their engagement just hours after the Queen and the Prince of Wales had been told.
The couple will marry next spring or summer in a ceremony that will attract one of the biggest worldwide TV audiences since the Prince of Wales married Lady Diana Spencer in 1981.
While Prince William insisted

Middleton's brother and sister were told little more than three hours before the announcement was made public.
Prince Harry, who also heard the news yesterday, said: "I am delighted that my brother has popped the question. It means I get a sister, which I have always wanted."
Asked why he had taken so many years to propose, the Prince said: "I didn't I was a man – but the time is right now, we're both very happy and I'm very glad that I have done it."
Miss Middleton said: "We have been going out for a long time and it just seemed the natural step for both of us."

got there
end

A ROYAL WAGER

The 2011 wedding of Prince William and Kate provides Brits with a chance to merge two popular pastimes: betting and Royal watching.

"There's a real tradition of betting on what the royals will do next," Darren Haines, a spokesman for bookmaker Paddy Power, told The Associated Press. "The U.K. has a strange fascination with the royals."

For years, Brits placed wagers on if, when, and where the couple would marry. With answers to those questions now firmly in hand, betting firms like Paddy Power and Ladbrokes began taking bets on other details of the couple's nuptials and married life:

How long will the train on Kate's wedding dress be?

Will Kate wear Jimmy Choo shoes?

Will Kate walk into Westminster Abbey on time?

Will the words "honor" and "obey" be included in Kate's vows?

Who will Prince Harry will take to the wedding as his date?

Will the couple make it to their 10th anniversary?

While some say it's in poor taste to bet on the failure of a marriage even before the couple has made it to the altar, bookmakers say they use good judgment on such matters. A wager on the likelihood of a terrorist attack the day of the ceremony, for example, was rejected.

"We don't look to bet on any-

thing that's distasteful so we refused that request," said Paddy Power's Haines. With the average bet on such matters hovering around the equivalency of $5, it's clear that Royal wagering is not about reaping huge rewards.

"This is all about fun," he said.

U.K. online bookmaker William Hill admits it took a substantial hit in November 2010 – £34,672 or roughly $55,000 – in payouts to gamblers who bet William and Kate would be married in April. The firm said it sustained a loss of nearly $320,000 when the engagement was announced.

CHAPTER SEVEN:

Royal Weddings in Other Lands

CHAPTER SEVEN: Royal Weddings in Other Lands

News about Prince William and Kate Middleton's engagement spread quickly; within minutes of their official announcement, the British media was abuzz. But the news didn't stop at the nation's borders.

Very soon after, the international press had sent news of the impending nuptials around the world. Bloggers, Twitter, and Facebook relayed the news to those who prefer to keep up on world events via less traditional means.

No doubt, modern-day information seekers are interested in the details of royal life – particularly when it comes to royal wed-

In countries with no monarchy, there's a certain wistfulness in regard to royalty.

dings. But why? And why do British royal couples seem to command more attention than those in other countries?

Media expert Jo Grobel told German broadcasting company Deutsche Wells that it's a matter of compensation.

In countries with no monarchy – like the United States, Mexico, Germany, and many others – there's a certain wistfulness in regard to royalty.

"We need the English to let us borrow a bit of theirs," she said. "That way, at least, we have a kind of secondhand royal court."

Pop culture expert Elayne Rapping, professor emerita of sociology at the State University of New York at Buffalo, agreed with Grobel, noting that movie stars are the closest thing Americans have to royalty and they tend to hold private ceremonies.

"Weddings in America (tend) to be kept private. Funerals seem to be bigger events in this country," she told the *Pittsburgh Tribune-Review*.

Royal families, with their coronations, ceremony, and crowns, have a sense of tradition that isn't present in countries where politicians are elected. Many Americans, for example, look to the formality and extravagance of a royal wedding to feel connected to the grand sense of European culture.

Rapping said Americans "love a good Cinderella story," reiterating the fact that Kate is the first commoner to marry an heir to the British throne since 1660. And, she noted, it doesn't hurt that Prince William and Middleton are attractive and personable.

The British Royal Family has long been a source of inspiration for films, television shows, and even soap operas, all of which has added to its intrigue. Princess Diana brought an enormous amount of drama to the royal story, beginning with her storybook wedding, continuing on through reports of her loveless marriage, and culminating with her tragic death in 1997.

"There is already speculation over whether or not Kate Middleton will be the next Diana – whether or not she'll also meet a tragic end," Grobel said. "In other words, it's good entertainment."

Royal weddings also provide a break from more sober news coverage of terrorist acts, economic crises and natural disasters.

Royal Romance, Modern Marriage

"People want something positive in between," Grobel said.

While the world's attention currently is focused on the British royal wedding, royalty in other countries have hosted some very spectacular, tradition-filled nuptials. Here's a quick look at the recent weddings of a handful of other royals:

The Princess & the Gym Owner

Sweden's four-day royal wedding celebration reached its peak on June 19, 2010, when Crown Princess Victoria married commoner Daniel Westling at Stockholm Cathedral. Gym-owner Westling met the princess nine years earlier, when he became her personal trainer.

Victoria is the oldest child of King Carl XVI Gustaf and Queen Silvia. She is in line to become Sweden's first female regent since Ulrika Eleonora, who reigned in the early 1700s.

The couple's 3:30 p.m. wedding was held at Stockholm's Storkyrkan Cathedral. The ceremony was attended by European royalty, including Queen Margrethe and Prince Consort Henrik of Denmark, Queen Sofia of Spain, King Harald and Queen Sonja of Norway, Queen Beatrix of the Netherlands, Princess Martha Louise of Norway and her husband Ari Behn, Princess Laurentien and Prince Constantijn of Holland, Crown Princess Mary and Crown Prince Frederik of Denmark, and Princess Madeleine of Sweden.

The couple emerged from their hour-long ceremony to a gauntlet of crossed swords, stepped into a horse-drawn carriage, and rode through town to the cheers of thousands of people lining the streets.

Upon their arrival at Stockholm's harbor, they boarded a gilt longboat driven by 18 naval oarsmen. The couple stood on the back of the boat waving to sailors saluting from ships and a submarine as they made their way across the harbor. The festivities continued with a formation of 16 fighter

jets performing a flyby as the royal boat approached the royal palace boat landing, crowded with sailors and cheering civilians.

The king and queen hosted a formal wedding banquet in the evening at the royal palace.

Post-wedding, Westling is known as Prince Daniel, Duke of Vaestergoetland, the palace announced.

CHAPTER SEVEN: Royal Weddings in Other Lands

Formality in France

France's Prince Jean d'Orleans, Duke of Vendome, and Philomena de Tornos were married in a religious ceremony on May 2, 2009. The couple had already been wed in a civil ceremony in Paris on March 19, 2009.

Prince Jean is the son of Henri Philippe, the Count of Paris, who is the claimant to the French throne from the House of Orléans. In 2006, Jean was named Dauphin of France, which was the traditional title for the heir to the French crown. Philomena is the daughter of United Nations diplomat Alfonso de Tornos.

The couple's religious ceremony drew crowds of well-wishers outside Senlis Cathedral in Senlis, France, all hoping for a glimpse of the royal couple. Philomena looked glamorous in a Christian Lacroix gown accented with gold embroidery and a lace-edged veil which clung to her turquoise tiara.

Members of many European royal houses attended the ceremony including Prince Guillaume and Sybille of Luxembourg, the Duke and Duchess of Wurtemberg, and Prince Philippe and Mathilde of Belgium. Following the exchange of vows, the newlyweds toasted their marriage with champagne with their guests in the gardens of Chateau d'Hugues Capet. The wedding party then moved on to a reception in the Chateau de Chantilly, where they were greeted with a wedding cake adorned with sparklers.

Prince Jean had previously been engaged to marry Duchess Tatjana of Oldenburg, but the 2001 wedding was cancelled because of a dispute over religion. The engagement was broken because the duchess did not want to convert to Catholicism.

Reportedly, Prince Jean's father feared his son's claim to the French throne would be in jeopardy if he produced a Protestant heir.

Big Fat Greek Wedding

Officially, the Greek monarchy ended in 1974 as the result of a military action and later referendum. However, when Prince Nikolaos of Greece and Denmark married on August 25, 2010, in Spetses, Greece, the wedding went on in true royal fashion.

Nikolaos is the second son of Constantine, the former king of Greece and his wife, Anne Marie. He married former fashion events planner Tatiana Blatnik, who is now known as Princess Nikolaos of Greece.

Princess Nikolaos is the granddaughter of Ellinka, Countess von Einsiedel.

The couple wed at sunset in the whitewashed 19th-century cathedral of Saint Nicholas. The groom arrived at the wedding by boat. The bride was chauffeured to the church in a horse-drawn carriage and was breathtaking in an ivory Angel Sanchez lace gown, antique corsage tiara and full-length veil.

Around 350 guests were in attendance including members of the Spanish royal family, Crown Princess Victoria of Sweden and husband Prince Daniel, representatives from the Norwegian, Dutch, and British royal families, Greek shipping heirs Stavros and Eugenie Niarchos, and singer Sir Elton John.

Yachts had been pulling up at Spetses, a small island in the Saronic Gulf, for days leading up to the royal wedding, with many tourists trying to get a glimpse of the newlyweds.

A Banker Becomes A Princess

Netherlands Crown Prince Willem-Alexander was in formal naval uniform and Argentine economist Maxima Zorreguieta wore a white Valentino gown when the two wed February 2, 2002, in Amsterdam. Willem-Alexander is the eldest of Queen Beatrix's three children.

Before a gallery of kings, queens, dukes, and counts, the couple first exchanged vows in a civil ceremony. Later the same day, they repeated their pledge to "love, honor, and obey" in a church ceremony officiated by a Dutch Reformed minister and a Catholic priest.

The church ceremony was followed by a half-hour ride through the heart of Amsterdam in the gilded carriage that carried Willem-Alexander's great-grandmother, Queen Wilhelmina, to her wedding 100 years earlier. The two-mile procession was led by more than 200 police and royal grenadiers on foot and on horseback, passing through a cordon of hundreds of salut-

CHAPTER SEVEN: Royal Weddings in Other Lands

ing soldiers and veterans.

Thousands of spectators waved Dutch flags and cheered the handsome couple. The streets were a sea of orange, the color of the ruling House of Orange. Citizens, many of whom slept overnight in Dam Square, wore orange hats, scarves, and plastic crowns.

The bride's parents did not attend the wedding. Maxima's father, Jorge Zorreguieta, was asked to stay away because of public discomfort over his association with the repressive Argentine regime of the 1970s and 1980s. The minister acknowledged her family, saying they were "today united in spirit with their daughter and son-in-law."

In addition to well-wishers, the wedding attracted around 1,000 protesters, some of whom urged dismantling The Netherlands' constitutional monarchy, while others demonstrated against the human rights abuses during the period Zorreguieta was in the Argentine government.

The Buenos Aires-born Maxima was working as an investment banker in New York when she met Willem-Alexander at a party in Spain. Almost as soon as the couple's engagement was announced, the Dutch people embraced Maxima with many commentators comparing her popularity to the late Princess Diana. The week of the royal wedding, a number of two-story-high banners were draped on many Amsterdam buildings proclaiming: "We Love You Maxima."

Maxima was granted dual citizenship – Dutch and Argentine – and, although she remains a Catholic, promised to raise her children Protestant.

Prince Willem-Alexander and Princess Maxima now have three daughters: Princess Catharina-Amalia, Princess Alexia, and Princess Ariane.

Choosing Love Over Royal Status

Japan's Princess Sayako lost her royal status in November 2005, when she married commoner Yoshiki Kuroda, in a ceremony in Tokyo.

The ceremony took place in Tokyo's Imperial Hotel and was attended by 30 people, making it quite informal and intimate by royal standards. Wearing a Western-style white dress and pearls, the princess sipped sake rice wine with her new husband.

Thousands of well-wishers lined the streets between the royal palace and the city hotel where the half-hour marriage rite took place.

Princess Sayako is Emperor Akihito's only daughter; she became the nation's first princess to abandon her title in 45 years. Post-wedding, the former princess is known as Sayako Kuroda. In addition to taking on a less regal new name, Sayako lost her royal allowance. She also had to learn to shop for groceries and drive a car – tasks many commoners take for granted.

Sayako and Kuroda, a descendant of Japan's now-abolished aristocracy, were childhood acquaintances. Their romance began in 2003, when the two attended a tennis party thrown by one of Sayako's brothers.

BRITISH ROYALTY ON FILM

When the dramatic film *The King's Speech* opened in late 2011, Oscar talk immediately followed.

The period piece tells the story of King George VI. When his older brother abdicates the throne, George "Bertie" VI (played by Colin Firth) reluctantly accepts the crown. Though his stutter raises concerns about his leadership skills, an unconventional speech therapist (portrayed by Geoffrey Rush) helps him find his voice and come into his own as a man and a ruler.

Filmgoers who know a thing or two about British history understand that *The King's Speech* is not a documentary but rather a dramatized tale intended to sell movie tickets and entertain the masses. The film was released just two years after *The Young Victoria* earned three Oscar nominations and after actress Helen Mirren won the Academy Award in 2006 for portraying the late king's daughter in *The Queen*.

This rapid-fire release of royal-related films begs the question: Is there no limit to Hollywood's fascination with the British monarchy?

"How long before we are treated to a film about George V's love affair with his stamps?" movie critic Dominic Sandbrook wrote in the (London) *Telegraph*.

No actors have yet been tied to such a film, but at least one other royal movie is headed to the big screen in coming months – and it's being directed by none-other-than actress/singer Madonna.

W.E, set for release in 2011, stars James D'Arcy, Abbie Cornish, Oscar Isaac and Andrea Riseborough. The film tells the parallel stories of the love affair between King Edward VIII and American divorcee Wallis Simpson, which led to the royal's abdication, and the contemporary story of a woman, Wally Winthrop, whose obsession with the life of the Duchess of Windsor guides her through her own romantic challenges.

These movies are part of an ongoing trend toward big-screen portrayals of life within the British monarchy. Here's a look at a few more:

The Young Victoria (2009): This film is a dramatization of the turbulent first years of Queen Victoria's (played by Emily Blunt) rule and her romance with Prince Albert. The film also stars Rupert Friend and Miranda Richardson. *The Young Victoria* earned three Academy Award nominations and won for costume design.

The Other Boleyn Girl (2008): This tale of romance and betrayal stars Natalie Portman as Anne Boleyn and Scarlett Johansson as her sister, Mary. Both of these women are mistresses of King Henry VIII (played by Eric Bana) but only one can become his Queen. The supporting cast includes Kristin Scott Thomas and Jim Sturgess.

The Queen (2006): Helen Mirren won an Oscar for playing Queen Elizabeth II in this movie. This fictional account of the events that took place following the death of Diana offers a fascinating look at the nature of Royalty. Michael Sheen co-stars as Tony Blair, and James Cromwell also puts in an appearance.

Elizabeth (1998): Cate Blanchett was nominated for an Oscar for her role as Queen Elizabeth I. Taking the throne after the death of her half-sister, Elizabeth inherits a kingdom surrounded by enemies. She engages in a romance with Robert Dudley (played by Joseph Fiennes), fights off plots by everyone from the Duke of

Norfolk (Christopher Eccleston) to Pope Pius V (Sir John Gielgud), and gains the confidence necessary to declare herself "The Virgin Queen."

Her Majesty, Mrs. Brown (1998): Depressed after the death of her husband, Queen Victoria (portrayed by Judi Dench) is coaxed back into public life by John Brown (played by Billy Connolly), a servant of her late spouse. As their relationship intensifies, rumors circulate about their inappropriate relationship. This film earned an Oscar nomination for Dench.

Henry V (1989) – King Henry V (portrayed by Kenneth Branagh) is insulted by the King of France. As a result, he leads his army into battle against France; along the way, the king struggles with low morale among his troupes and his own self-doubts. In addition to starring, Branagh also directed and starred in this adaptation of William Shakespeare's play *The Life of Henry*

the Fifth.

Anne of the Thousand Days (1969) – This Oscar-winning film tells the story of Henry VIII (Richard Burton) who dumps his wife, Catherine of Aragon (Irene Papas), in favor of his mistress Anne Boleyn (portrayed by Genevieve Bujold). Anne's one-thousand-day-reign as Queen ends with the loss of her head.

The Lion in Winter (1968) – This movie, based on a Broadway play, follows King Henry II (Peter O'Toole) and Queen Eleanor (Katharine Hepburn) as they gather on Christmas in 1183 and begin to bicker over who should be the next ruler. A complete work of fiction, the story is nonetheless an entertaining tale of love, power, and intrigue. A 2003 made-for-TV remake of this film starred Patrick Stewart and Glenn Close.

Young Bess (1953) – Fully intending to capitalize upon the public's fascination of royal life, MGM released this film to coincide with the June 2, 1953, crowning of Queen Elizabeth II. In this movie, young Elizabeth (portrayed by Jean Simmons) is in danger after her mother, Anne Boleyn (Elaine Stewart), is executed. This lavish film focuses on the story of Elizabeth's brother, Edward, whose death cleared the way for her to become queen. The movie is based on a book by Margaret Irwin.

The Private Life of Henry VIII (1933) – Charles Laughton won the Academy Award for his portrayal of Henry, who famously married six different queens, divorcing or beheading them at his discretion. Wendy Barrie, Binnie Barnes, Everly Gregg, Merle Oberon, Robert Donat, and Laughton's real-life wife Elsa Lanchester also star. This was the first British film to be nominated for the Academy Award for Best Picture.

CHAPTER EIGHT:

Welcome to the Family

CHAPTER EIGHT: Welcome to the Family

Any new marriage brings with it a period of adjustment. There's often a combining of households. You have to divvy up chores, decide who will sleep on which side of the bed, figure out finances, and embrace an entirely new set of family traditions.

When you marry into the British

Royal Family, you need to multiply those adjustments by about 1,000. There is no denying that Kate Middleton is going to have a steep learning curve when it comes to grasping the intricacies of Royal life.

To help her adjust to her new role and responsibilities, Sophie Countess of Wessex has agreed to be Kate's personal mentor. The Countess is the wife of Prince Edward, Earl of Wessex. Sophie is reportedly the first of the Queen's children-in-law to have an ongoing, warm relationship with Her Majesty; the two share many interests, including horses and military history.

The Countess' own transition into the royal family was a bumpy one. She kept her public relations job after her royal wedding but, in 2001, a tabloid reporter recorded her saying disparaging things about government officials and appearing to use her royal status in order to gain business clients. In an attempt to counter the bad publicity, the Countess agreed to an interview about her fertility issues with that same tabloid magazine. The Royal Family was embarrassed, however, when the published article was titled "My Edward's Not Gay." Soon after, Sophie quit her private sector job and began focusing her time on royal duties.

Those life challenges have taught the Countess plenty and it's those insider bits of wisdom she'll likely be sharing with Kate.

Beyond the Countess' mentoring and guidance, Miss Middleton reportedly has received counseling in preparation for her

Sophie, Countess of Wessex and Prince Edward, Earl of Wessex pose for a photograph following a visit to Whitton School on June 19, 2009.

Pomp and ceremony are an integral part of royal life. Left to right, Prince Andrew, Duke of York, Prince William and Prince Edward, Earl of Wessex, attend the Order of the Garter Ceremony at Windsor Castle in June 2010.

new role as a royal. *The (London) Daily Mail* reported that plans initiated by Prince William called for Kate to have "training sessions" to help her avoid the depression and isolation felt by Princess Diana.

And, as if mentoring and counseling weren't enough, since mid-2005 Prince William's fiancée also has been receiving lessons in etiquette and protocol, and in the complex workings of the monarchy.

To say the Royal Family is complicated is a bit of an understatement. Even among members of the family, it's not always clear who is and is not considered an official member of the Royals.

Kate will have her hands full just figuring out the Royal Household, which has five departments: the Private Secretary's Office, the Master of the Household's Department, the Privy Purse and Treasurer's Office, the Lord Chamberlain's Office, and the Royal Collection Department.

Most of the Departments are based at Buckingham Palace, although staff also work at St. James's Palace, Windsor Castle, the Palace of Holyroodhouse and the Royal Mews. Some Royal Household employees also travel with the Queen on overseas visits and during the Queen's stay at Balmoral Castle and Sandringham.

Just keeping all those palaces and castles straight is enough to make a

Parade at Windsor Castle.

Balmoral castle.

princess' head spin.

Throughout the centuries, Britain's kings and queens have built or purchased palaces to serve as family homes and offices. Kate may need a map to keep them all straight. Each of the residences still standing fits into one of three classifications: official royal residences held in trust for future generations (Buckingham Palace and Windsor Castle are the best known of these); private estates owned by the Queen and used to generate income through farming or tours (Balmoral Castle and Sandringham House, for example); and unoccupied royal residences which once housed members of the Royal Family and are, consequently, of historical interest. Additionally, the Historical Royal Palaces are a specific set of former Royal residences owned by the Queen on behalf of the nation and run by an independent charity; these palaces are the Tower of London, Hampton Court Palace, the Banqueting House, Kensingston Palace, and Kew Palace.

There's so much to learn about coronations and curtseying, palaces and public appearances that it's certain Kate's royal training and mentorship will continue long after her wedding day.

"Kate is not joining the Windsor dynasty to be a princess, she's joining to be a queen at some point in the future," Patrick Jephson, former private secretary to Princess Diana, told the Associated Press. "There's a lot at stake here, more than just pretty dresses and magazine covers. You have to show that the dynasty can renew and rejuvenate itself."

For Kate Middleton, her fairytale wedding is just the beginning. She's being welcomed into the Royal Family with open arms. Whether she can wear the crown comfortably and with confidence will be up to her.

Sandringham House and gardens.

Given her "common" heritage, Kate Middleton is receiving lessons in etiquette and royal protocol by her own private mentor, the Countess of Wessex.

SINGING ABOUT THE QUEEN

Her Majesty's a pretty nice girl,
but she doesn't have a lot to say
Her Majesty's a pretty nice girl
but she changes from day to day

The Sex Pistols released "God Save the Queen" in 1977. The controversial single's lyrics suggested there was "no future" and compared England to a "fascist regime."

The English rock band The Smiths released the song and album "The Queen Is Dead" in 1986, a lyrical criticism of the monarchy. The Pet Shop Boys released a track called "Dreaming of the Queen" in 1993:

Dreaming of the Queen
Visiting for tea.
You and her and I
And Lady Di.
The Queen said: "I'm aghast
Love never seems to last,
However hard you try"

Queen Elizabeth II was crowned in 1953. Her reign, one of the longest for a British monarch, has provided inspiration for authors, poets, filmmakers and, yes, songwriters. Some of the lyrics are flattering other, quite simply, are not.

"Her Majesty," written by Paul McCartney and featured on the Beatles' 1969 album *Abbey Road*, pays homage to the Queen. McCartney played the song at the Party at the Palace concert during the Golden Jubilee in 2002:

English alternative rock band the Stone Roses included a song about the Queen on their 1989 debut album. Set to the tune of "Scarborough Faire," the tart, 59-second tune declares:

Tear me apart and boil my bones,
I'll not rest till she's lost her throne.
My aim is true my message is clear,
It's curtains for you, Elizabeth my dear.

UNCOMMON COMMONERS

For centuries, monarchies have had rules – some written, some implied – that required the monarch and those in the line of succession to marry a spouse from a royal or at least noble family. Often, royal families arranged marriages to strengthen the influence of the royal house by making strategic alliances.

That Kate Middleton's parents are common business owners has sparked debate around the world. Some believe Prince William and Kate's marriage will breathe new life into the monarchy. Others fear the Royal Family's influence will be diminished by her presence.

Regardless of how she's viewed, it should be noted Kate is not the first commoner to marry a future king.

Grand Duchess Maria Teresa of Luxembourg, Queen Sonja of Norway, and Empress Michiko of Japan were all commoners who married into the current generation of the world's royalty. These women had trouble gaining respect within their royal houses and, as a result, struggled for acceptance.

Conversely, Queen Silvia of Sweden, Queen Rania of Jordan, and Lalla Salma of Morocco were all commoners whose royal marriages are thought to have strengthened their monarchies.

Silvia Sommerlath was raised in an international family; her father was a businessman from Germany and her mother was from Brazil, where Silvia spent most of her childhood. She met Sweden's Crown Prince Carl Gustaf during the 1972 Summer Olympics in Munich, a year before he became King Carl XVI Gustaf. After secretly dating for four years, Silvia and Carl Gustaf were married in 1976. At the time, the new King of Sweden's future did not look promising. Sweden was on the verge of becoming a republic, and Carl Gustaf lacked both charisma and drive. With her charm and abilities in languages (she had been an interpreter before meeting Carl Gustaf), Silvia overcame these problems to win the hearts of the public.

Rania Al-Jasin was born in Kuwait to Palestinian parents. She met and married Prince Abdullah bin Al-Hussein of Jordan in 1993. Prince Abdullah had been pursuing a military career when his father, King Hussein I of Jordan, named him the Crown Prince. Just two weeks later, the King died and Abdullah became king. Unlike low-key Arabian queens before her, Rania was not content to stand in her husband's shadow. Rania put her college education and good looks to work, creating a role for herself that champions issues related to children and women's rights. Despite her Palestinian origins she's loved by the Jordanian people and has become one of the world's most recognizable queens.

When Lalla Salma married Morocco's King Mohammed VI in 2002, she became the first wife of a Moroccan ruler to be publicly acknowledged and given a royal title. Although it is not known where the couple met, their marriage was not arranged. Lalla Salma – born Salma Bennani – was an excellent student, earning a degree in computer science. As a princess consort who has managed to live a modern life while still respecting Morocco's culture and traditions, she has become a role model and inspiration for modern women in Morocco. Lalla Salma carries out her own royal duties and assists her husband in representing Morocco.

THEY SAID WHAT?

"*Like all the best families, we have our share of eccentricities, of impetuous and wayward youngsters and of family disagreements.*"
– Queen Elizabeth II

"*Being a princess isn't all it's cracked up to be.*"
– Princess Diana

"*When I appear in public people expect me to neigh, grind my teeth, paw the ground and swish my tail – none of which is easy.*"
– Princess Anne

"*I believe passionately that everyone has a particular God-given ability.*"
– Prince Charles

"*I am and always will be an HRH. But out of personal choice I like to be called William because that is my name and I want people to call me William – for now.*"
– Prince William

"*People say to me, 'Would you like to swap your life with me for 24 hours? Your life must be very strange.' But of course I have not experienced any other life. It's not strange to me.*"
– Prince Andrew

"*It was dreadful. They tried to put the little redhead in a cage.*"
– Sarah Ferguson

"*The problem I have with the press is that if you tell them anything interesting, they never take any notice.*"
– Zara Phillips, daughter of Princess Anne and Captain Mark Philips

"*If you travel as much as we do, you appreciate how much more aircraft have become. Unless you travel in something called economy class, which sounds ghastly.*"
– Prince Philip

"*I have the heart of a man, not a woman, and I am not afraid of anything.*"
– Queen Elizabeth I

"*Within our private life and within certain other parts of our life we want to be as normal as possible. ... It's hard, because to a certain respect we never will be normal.*"
– Prince Harry

"*He's lucky to be going out with me.*"
– Kate Middleton

"*I have as much privacy as a goldfish in a bowl.*"
– Princess Margaret

"*The important thing is not what they think of me, but what I think of them.*"
– Queen Victoria

CHAPTER NINE:

Charitably Royal

CHAPTER NINE: Charitably Royal

When Prince Charles and Diana got married in 1981, they received more than 6,000 wedding presents from well-wishers around the world. Among the gifts? A roomful of antique furniture from the people of Canada, 20 engraved silver platters from Australia, an engraved porcelain set from President Ronald Reagan.

A selection of Charles and Diana's wedding gifts were placed on display to members of the public at St James's Palace and some items were later distributed to charities chosen by Charles.

Prince William and Kate Middleton will certainly receive gifts but, in a preemptive strike, they're asking guests to their wedding to forgo a present in favor of a charitable donation.

The British Royal family has a long history of charitable giving dating back to the

Prince Charles' charitable foundation raises more than $160 million annually for good causes.

18th century. The first recorded patronage was George II's involvement with the Society of Antiquaries, a group concerned with architecture and art history.

Between them, members of the *Royal Family* hold approximately 3,000 patronages of charitable organizations. Patronages generally reflect the interests of the member of the Royal Family involved.

Queen Elizabeth II is patron of more than 600 charities including CRUSE Bereavement Services, I CAN (which helps children with speech and language difficulties), the Royal Agricultural Benevolent Institution, and the Soldier, Sailors, and Air Force Association.

In late 2010, Prince Charles' group of charities – collectively known as The Prince's Charities Foundation – came under scrutiny regarding its high operational costs. Still, the Prince's charity empire, which typically raises more than £100 million (around $160 million) annually for good causes, is described by his aides as "the largest multi-cause charitable enterprise in the UK." Eighteen of the charities were founded personally by the Prince.

From the moment Diana's engagement to Prince Charles was announced, Diana embraced the Royal Family's commitment to charitable causes – often in bold and image-shattering ways. Her work with victims of AIDS could be viewed in this regard. She was one of the first high-profile people photographed touching AIDS victims; those images had a significant impact in changing people's attitudes about the disease. The princess not only raised funds on behalf of her charities but also served the needy and inspired others to follow her lead.

Prince William currently is focused on his military career but is following in his parents' footsteps by showing his support for organizations that support issues he cares about.

New York

CHAPTER NINE: Charitably Royal

William is patron of several organizations including the Tusk Trust, a conservation charity for wildlife in Africa, and Centrepoint, the United Kingdom's leading charity for the homeless, of which his late mother was also the patron.

In 2007, Prince William became president of the Royal Marsden Hospital, a position previously held by the Princess of Wales. The Prince had visited the hospital a number of times and, in 2005, undertook two days of work experience there.

The Prince is president of the Football Association, the governing body of English football, and patron of Mountain Rescue England and Wales and the English Schools' Swimming Association. The patronages reflect William's interest in youth sports and, in his own words, a desire to "highlight and celebrate the vital, selfless and courageous work of our mountain rescue organizations."

Prince William is patron of Skill Force, a charity that uses the skills of former members of the Armed Forces to run life skills courses for disadvantaged young people. As a tribute to his grandmother, he also became patron of The Queen Elizabeth II Fields, an initiative run by Fields in Trust to protect and create hundreds of playing fields throughout the UK in honor of Queen Elizabeth II's Diamond Jubilee in 2012.

In 2009, Prince William and Prince Harry created their own foundation to further their charitable efforts. The princes' charity will provide grants to needy young people, wounded servicemen and women, and for sustainable development, both at home and overseas. They announced they would give at least a third of all the money raised by the foundation to the welfare of the military, a cause championed by their father and grandmother. Newspapers reported that the brothers invested a six figure sum of their personal fortune to create the foundation.

Now that Kate is becoming an official part of the Royal Family, she, too, is a sought-after patron for many worthy causes. Months before the wedding, palace spokespeople confirmed they had already begun receiving requests for Kate's charitable backing.

It will take "months or even years," for her to gradually build up her set of patronages, a palace source told *People* magazine.

"Inevitably we have had approaches, but we are not making decisions before the wedding," the spokesman said. "Catherine wants time, once she is a member of the Royal Family, to come to a decision about what she wants to do. She wants to decide what her own interests are and develop those over time."

Prior to the royal wedding, Kate supported several fundraising events for Starlight, a charity which grants wishes to seriously and terminally ill children. It was widely reported she was considering a request to work as its patron or ambassador after her nuptials.

Developing her own charitable life will be among Kate's royal obligations but she's interested in exploring her many options before committing.

Said the royal spokesman: "She wants to do something that she is genuinely passionate about."

COULD WILLS' DAUGHTER BECOME QUEEN?

With Prince William and Kate Middleton's wedding still months away, Commonwealth leaders were deep in conversation about whether they should update the law of succession to the British throne.

300-year-old Act of Settlement discriminates against women. But changing the law would be complicated and would require each of the 15 Commonwealth countries to adopt the same amendment.

Keith Vaz, Labour MP, is leading the charge to change the existing law noting that laws governing the British Royal Family should be modernized.

"The law is outdated in the 21st century, where people expect that discrimination of any kind should not exist and there should be equality regardless of race, gender, or religion," Vaz told the *International Business Times*.

According to current law, if Wills and Kate have a daughter and then a son, the daughter would get passed over and the son would become King.

Government leaders admit the

Vaz and others view the wedding of William and Kate as a once-in-a-generation opportunity to change the law.